Messed Up Ministries
Presents

40 Cups of Coffee
A Devotional Guide from the Minister of Mocha

Written by Paul Pippen
Editors: Bev Pippen, Giselle Gatdula, Heather Cantori and Paul Pippen

Copyright © 2025 Paul Pippen
All rights reserved

No part of this book may be reproduced, or stored in a retrieval system, or transmitted in any form or by any means, electronic, mechanical, photocopying, recording, or otherwise, without express written permission of the publisher.
ISBN: 9798309328444
Edited by: Beverly Pippen, Giselle Gatdula, & Paul Pippen
Interior and Exterior Fonts: Arial
Photos and Images: Paul Pippen
Latte art courtesy of Cydney Browning
Design: Paul Pippen
Exterior Photos: Kristen Honeywell
Scripture quotations taken from The Holy Bible, New International Version® NIV® Copyright © 1973, 1978, 1984, 2011 by Biblica, Inc. TM Used by permission. All rights reserved worldwide.

Printed in the United States of America

for Dan, Ryan, "Guitar" Mark and Steve…

Table of Contents

Foreword	1
Introduction	3
Day 1	9
Day 2	13
Day 3	17
Day 4	19
Day 5	23
Day 6	27
Day 7	31
Day 8	35
Day 9	39
Day 10	43
Day 11	47
Day 12	51
Day 13	55
Day 14	59

Day 15	63
Day 16	67
Day 17	69
Day 18	73
Day 19	75
Day 20	79
Day 21	83
Day 22	87
Day 23	91
Day 24	93
Day 25	97
Day 26	101
Day 27	107
Day 28	111
Day 29	115
Day 30	119
Day 31	123
Day 32	125
Day 33	129

Day 34	133
Day 35	137
Day 36	141
Day 37	145
Day 38	149
Day 39	153
Day 40	157
Afterword	159
About the Author	161
More from Paul Pippen	163

Foreword

by Todd Black

I'll never forget the first appointment on my calendar after becoming the pastor of my new church. It took incredible courage and vulnerability for Paul and Bev to share what had transpired years earlier in Paul's life. He spoke openly about the process of healing and restoration that God had worked in him, and it was clear, Paul was a changed man.

Over the weeks and months that followed, I got to know Paul on a deeper level. I saw his heart and passion to share his story, encouraging others to experience the same life-changing transformation he had.

I've never met anyone as persistent and disciplined as Paul in pursuing what he sets out to accomplish. These qualities have allowed him to document both the highs and lows of his everyday life and share them with others. Paul speaks with honesty, humor, and a message of hope—that no matter how messy life gets, it can be turned into something meaningful.

Whether he's reflecting on life's greatest joys or its hardest lessons, you can't help but relate to him. His story is a reminder that we're not alone in our struggles, and even in the messiest moments, there's purpose to be found.

As you read, I'm confident you'll find something that resonates with you. Whether it's something that makes you stop and reflect, laugh, or maybe even shed a tear.

Congratulations, Paul, on accomplishing what you set out to do. Keep up the great work!

Introduction

40

We find the number 40 throughout our world and history. I'm no numerologist, but I am ok at looking for patterns. God has used the number 40 several times. It would have been really cool to find 40 references to 40, but alas, I just don't have the time or energy for such a project.

Most of us are familiar with Noah and the flood. Rain for 40 days and nights. That's a lot of rain. I think even a week would make a point, but leave it to our God to use some italics! 40 days and nights of rain; a creation flooded out entirely; now that is the way to make your point.

But seriously, God is pretty powerful. He could have done anything he wanted. He could have made a shield of protection around Noah and his menagerie, then flexed his power and zapped the rest of the creators into non-existence. He could have done the ultimate Jedi Mind Trick and just eradicated what he wanted gone. He could have done what I keep doing: select and delete the text. One mouse click on the left side of Noah, shift-click on the right side of the zebras, then delete. Poof! It's all gone, almost like it was never there.

Jesus and Moses both spent 40 days in seclusion in order to get closer to God and to find clarity about their mission and ministry. Burning bushes and temptation from the Enemy aside, that's more time than I've spent alone in a desert, and I've lived in one for essentially my entire life.

In the movie Spinal Tap there is a famous scene where guitarist Nigel Tufnel gives a brief tour of his extensive collection of equipment. He proudly shows that one of the amps "goes to 11". Moses did his "11" in 40's. He had three distinct 40 year periods in his life. I've never met Moses, but my teaching instinct leads me to believe that he just might have been a bit stubborn. You might even label him as "uncoachable". He needed 40 years of wandering in the desert. From the age of 40 until he was 80 he wandered the wilderness in order for God to temper him. *Italics* and **bold face**!

I'm in the later part of my 50's and I can't imagine needing that long to get it, but check out what comes next. Yup, 40 more years of desert wandering, only this time with a group of unhappy refugees. ***Italics,***

bold face, and an increase in font size! God has His methods. All I can say is that I'm glad to not be Moses!

Yet we see 40 in more places than just that. In 1983 the band U2 was working on their third studio album. At that point they had a minor following, but certainly nothing like what they have now. Faced with a lack of one song and running out of time in the studio they created a song titled 40. The song is based on the 40th Psalm, and while it wasn't a major hit, it became a staple of live shows back in the day.

Yup, 40 is significant.

So at some point in 2024 I found myself looking at a calendar and realized that the *Minister of Mocha* blog was turning 10 years old in February of 2025. That's a pretty good run.

Ostensibly, the blog started as a way to promote our new Celebrate Recovery meeting. I was running a nascent media department at my church. Like so many things I have done, it kind of came together without a lot of forethought. I often ask "Is it odd or is it God?" and this definitely fits in with that line of inquiry.

I was volunteering at the church and things just sort of evolved. Following the leading of God, I began creating video content. Blogs became a vehicle to try and drive traffic to the videos. I started many blogs (not 40, but wouldn't that have been just the thing?!?) for myself and others. This is the one that stuck.

Focusing on recovery issues and trying to just provide a little blast of hope for people at the beginning of their work week was the goal. At some point I landed on the tagline of "Rise Up". I thought I had used it from the start, but as I read through 500+ blog entries I found out that it wasn't there back in February of 2015.

Coffee, recovery, and writing have all been important tools in getting me through my sometimes stormy life. I write these things and post them for the world to see, but my target audience is me. I've never planned them out in advance. They essentially represent a stream of consciousness on any given Monday morning in my life over the past 10 years. It's a bit of a historical road map and a bit of a pep talk. It's me taking the thoughts rattling around in my head and trying to see what they look like out in the open. It might not always be wonderful, but it's always honest. I am thankful to all of the readers who have stopped in or stayed with me.

I would be remiss if I failed to acknowledge my friend and brother Dan Paxton. His role in all of this is important, because I took my moniker from him. He used it before I did. Since I do a lot of work in prisons, I won't say that I stole it from him. I'm sure you understand. Let's just say that he was gracious enough to allow my "tactical appropriation" of the name all those years ago.

So sit back and get ready for your very own 40 days. I encourage a cup of coffee and maybe a pastry to help you welcome each day. Perhaps some soft music in the background. That's the way I do it, but you do what you need to. Each day I'll give you the original text from a blog entry, then I will pair it with a Bible verse and some thoughts to help you with your devotions. All of the verses will be from the NIV unless I mention otherwise. Allow some time to ruminate on what you've read. Meditation is much more than a yoga pose and a mantra. Spend some time thinking about God in your life.

If you enjoy the book, I highly encourage you to go back and check out the blog. It comes out every

Monday morning California time. You can find it at MinisterOfMocha.com.

Ok, enough rambling, it's time to…

–Rise Up!!

Day 1

God's Hurricane (5.7.2018)

I've never been in a hurricane, but my wife grew up in South Florida so she knows the story well. I understand the science of them though. Here's a short lesson: the edges are not as bad, then as you get "deeper" into the storm it gets worse and worse, And then right in the middle is the eye. My wife tells me that she remembers everything going calm when the eye passed over. It was calm in the middle of the storm.

My walk in recovery is often that same hurricane. I wander around and feel the rush of the wind. I ignore the breeze, then it builds to a gale. The sprinkles become rain drops. The drops grow into driving sheets of water that begin to flood my world. The wind rips my life apart and strews my broken wreckage hither and yon. For a long time now I've been the idiot clinging to a tree. I've been the fool sitting on the roof watching the water rise. I've been "weathering the storm." Notice the nouns: idiot, fool, storm.

H

Good news! I have found the eye in the storm. God has me in the eye! The eye has peace. The eye has calm. The eye gives rest. It's wonderful! But that isn't the end of the story. I now have a choice: I can sit down and rest in the eye and just wait until the wrath returns on the other side of the eye. Yes, that's certainly one of my options.

Instead I am choosing to run in the eye. I choose to go the direction that God takes that eye and stay right there smack-dab in the middle of all that peace and beauty. If God goes right, Paul goes right. If God goes left, you guessed it, Paul goes left. And when I feel those winds coming back that is my warning that I am drifting from the eye. Will I sit or will I run? I think I will…

--Rise Up!!

================================

"You will keep in perfect peace those whose minds are steadfast, because they trust in you."
-Isaiah 26:3

Meditation thoughts:

What is the storm I am experiencing?
What is the next storm on the horizon?
How can I get into the calm of this storm?
Did I create this storm?
What comes after the storm?

Prayer:

"Dear Jesus, thank you for the storms in life. Thank you for guiding me through them. You are my guide. You are my shelter. Please keep my feet solidly in the eye of the storm. I pray this in the powerful name of Jesus, Amen."

Day 2

And The Winner Is...(2.25.2019)

Last night was a big night for cinema fans around the country, and even worldwide. The annual #AcademyAwards took place last night, with all of the requisite pomp and circumstance. Ladies wearing impossibly uncomfortable and impractical gowns smiling on a red carpet were only a part of the evening. Often, the winners follow the suspected script, but every once in a while an award is given to a person who obviously had no idea they would win. Those moments are my favorites. The thing about winning an #Oscar is that it will change how people see you forever. Before the win, you were you; after the win, the phrase "Oscar Winner" will become your new first name. It becomes something important that people will know you for and as.

I have done a lot of things, both noble and ignoble, that people try to use as a tag for me as well. My Oscar movement happened not when I accepted an award, but when I accepted Christ. He forever changed me and beyond all of my other history, that is what you need to know about me. I am a grateful Christian believer who struggles with co-dependency and my name is Paul. Did you catch it? I am not defined by my struggle, I'm defined by my faith in Jesus! The same holds true for you!

Now go and...

--Rise Up!!

===============================

"and you are of Christ, and Christ is of God."
-1 Corinthians 3:23

Meditation thoughts:
    What surprise victories have I had lately?
    What have I allowed to define me?
    What does my acceptance speech sound like?
    Is my speech written or will I wing it?

Prayer:

"Dear Jesus, thank you for the victories you provide. I accept the victories that you have given me and I accept the victories that are still coming for me in the future. I pray this in the powerful name of Jesus, Amen."

Day 3

Eagles and Crows (3.22.2021)

I recently heard about the eagle and the crow. It is said that the only bird that dares peck the eagle is the crow. All other birds are afraid of the powerful eagle, but the crow will land on the eagle's back and peck at its neck. Apparently the eagle does not fight back. Instead it takes flight with the crow on its back. It simply flies higher and higher. As it gains altitude the air gets thinner. The eagle is built for higher altitudes and can handle the lack of oxygen, but the crow cannot. Eventually, without a fight, the crow has to let go and fly back to a more comfortable altitude and the eagle is free of its tormentor.

Recovery is full of crows pecking at our necks, but we are all eagles. We don't need to accept the torment of our hurts, hang ups, and habits. We don't need to flail at the addictions and sins that try to trip us up. We need to trust that God made us better and soar higher than those troubles. When addiction comes to peck at your neck, get out of your nest and...

--Rise Up!!

==================================

"but those who hope in the Lord will renew their strength. They will soar on wings like eagles; they will run and not grow weary, they will walk and not be faint."

-Isaiah 40:31

Meditation thoughts:
    Am I a crow or am I an eagle?
    Do I fight back or do I fly higher?
    What happens when I come back to lower altitudes?

Prayer:
    "Dear Jesus, you are my wings. You give me all that I have, want, and need. Please protect me from attack and please give me the fortitude to fly higher when attacks do come my way. I pray this in the powerful name of Jesus, Amen."

Day 4

My Shirt (8.3.2015)

I went to put on a shirt the other day. Well, I guess I do that every day, but the day I'm thinking of was Saturday. We were headed down to my aunt's house for the annual family BBQ and I wanted to find the perfect shirt. I needed something that served multiple purposes: it needed to tell the story of my past year; it needed to be comfortable to wear in the car; it needed to be light colored so as to be comfortable in the sun. The shirt I chose was my very light cream colored (almost, but not quite white) Tommy Bahama shirt.

Normally I wouldn't have a Tommy Bahama shirt, but because my good friend Pastor Mark has lost about a gajillion pounds this year, I've been the recipient of his hand-me-downs, and the man dresses well!😀

Anyhow, I decided on this shirt because it seemed to meet the criteria point for point. Everything was going great until it came down to the time when the

food was put out. Me eating from a plate on my lap in a light colored shirt doesn't exactly scream success. I did fantastic on my first plate, but when I went back to get some (more) fruit salad my true talents presented themselves and splat, a blueberry fell from my fork and rolled down my chest leaving behind it a beautiful purple trail of remembrance.

I was left with a choice to make: what do you do with a stained shirt? Some people would suggest throwing the shirt out; some would wear it with pride; some would cover the stain with more clothing; some would stain the rest of the shirt so that the original stain was hidden; some would wash the stain out. I chose the latter.

A similar thing happened when Jesus was hanging out and his Paul got stained. Big choice to make here. Many people screamed to just throw him out. Others suggested that the sins that Paul commits are who he is and that he should just live and let live. There were those who thought that Paul's sins could be covered by a bunch of new behaviors that would cover the old ones without actually removing them. At one point Paul even thought that maybe going nuts and sinning all the time was a good answer, it's hard to tell one sin from another if they're everywhere. It's cool that Jesus had the "New and Improved" Covenant to use though. It turns out that it DID get those stains out, and returned Paul to the "white as snow" status!

When we sin, we should look at ourselves as that shirt. A stain or blemish is not a good reason to throw out the entire article. As I work my steps I can see Jesus doing my laundry. I suggest you let Him do it for you too. 24 hour service, no coins needed, fluff-and-fold included!

--Rise Up!!

================================

"'Come now, let us settle the matter,' says the Lord. 'Though your sins are like scarlet, they shall be as white as snow; though they are red as crimson, they shall be like wool.'"

-Isaiah 1:18

Meditation thoughts:
    What stains are on your "shirt"?
    How long have you worn your stains?
    Is your shirt ready for laundry or the trash?

Prayer:
"Dear Jesus, I have sinned many times in my life, but you are my redeemer. Thank you for making your sacrifice so that I would be as white as snow. Thank you for letting me be a living example of your love and forgiveness. I pray this in the powerful name of Jesus, Amen."

Day 5

Walls (3.28.2015)

Here I am again, still in Tennessee working on a house...last week it was digging ditches, this week we are hanging drywall on the walls. By now you probably can guess that it got me thinking about recovery!

When we went into the house another crew had already put up the studs for the dividing walls, but stud walls aren't exactly walls. We could and did walk right through them. We could move from "room" to "room" without finding the doors or halls. Sunshine came streaming throughout the whole house as did a pleasant, cooling breeze.

Then we "gone an' done it" (my Southernese is coming out after two weeks back in Nashville). As we started to put up the walls we began blocking out all those things that we were surrounded with before. The breeze began to fade. Our source of light diminished. We had to find new paths to get to the places we were going. At one point we had Pastor Mark boxed into a pantry with no light and no way out.

In recovery I often find that I have put up walls. I've created barriers to block out the things that hurt me. I've shut out the bad things, but oftentimes, I've shut out much of the good as well. I've found myself in the situation that Pastor Mark did. It seems good as I put up boundaries to shield me from the bad mistakes I am prone to make. It seems healthy to block out nouns (people, places, and things) that can cause me pain. But sometimes I get so overzealous that I find myself shut into a room with no windows and no doors. I'm inside and nothing can reach me, but I'm trapped all alone too.

So back to Pastor Mark. We quickly realized that we had pinned him in. Perhaps it was the moving of the Spirit; perhaps it was him banging on the wall. Either way, we got out the drywall saw and cut out around the door frame to let him out. That's just another reminder that any wall we build up can be taken down as well. I encourage all of us to take a look around and see if our boundaries have become jail cells. Just like walls in a home, it's good to have reasonable boundaries, but don't get yourself locked inside! Come out, then…

--Rise Up!!

================================

"When he had said this, Jesus called in a loud voice, 'Lazarus, come out!'"

-John 11:43

Meditation thoughts:
What nouns are you removing in your life?
Are you locked in the room or did you lock others into a room?
How long did it take to notice getting shut in?
Who are the people in your life who can help take down your walls?

Prayer:
"Dear Jesus, thank you for the shelter you provide. Please help me to find discernment as I eliminate some of the nouns in my life. I'm asking you to send people to help guide me in my walk. Please allow me to be weak enough to see their help as love and not an attack. I pray this in the powerful name of Jesus, Amen."

Day 6

Illin' (1.23.2017)

Last week I was sick...

I went to a hockey game with my family and my beloved Kings lost, so I was sick over that. Then I caught the creeping crud that has been making the rounds in Ridgecrest the past few weeks (or more truthfully it caught me!) and again, I was sick. I spent most of the week in bed wishing for the sickness to just take me or leave me, but to quit trying to strike up a long-term relationship with me!

I did all the right things. I prayed. I had others pray. I took the medicines. I drank the fluids. I got the rest. I called my daughters who are doctors. I even binge-watched lots of television. None of it worked. NONE OF IT!!! I stayed sick all week.

Then it happened...things began to change. I woke up on Friday and I was feeling a little better; then Saturday a little better than that; and each day since - better still.

Healing rarely happens instantaneously. Most of the time, even though we are doing the right things we need to give it time to work. Taking the medicine wasn't the hard part; waiting for it to work was. Getting rest wasn't the hard part; getting enough of it was. Drinking the fluids wasn't the hard part; waiting for my body to use them was. Submitting myself to prayer wasn't the hard part; accepting the slow answer was.

I'll always be illin' from something. That isn't the hard part; taking the time and effort to heal is.

--Rise Up!!

================================

"Not only so, but we also glory in our sufferings, because we know that suffering produces perseverance; perseverance, character; and character, hope. And hope does not put us to shame…"

-Romans 5:3-5a

Meditation thoughts:
How do I get well when I am sick?
Am I doing anything to stay healthy?
When I get sick do I push through or do I "give in" to the illness and rest?

Prayer:
> "Dear Jesus, you are the Healer. You are what I need when sickness takes over in my body and in my life. When I can go no further, you carry me forward. Thank you for healing me. Please heal my wounds and the things that ail me. I pray this in the powerful name of Jesus, Amen."

Day 7

Robocall (11.5.2018)

In this day in age, it is very likely that everyone who reads this has received a "robocall" at some point. A company or candidate pays a nominal fee and then a recorded message gets blasted out over the phone in our homes and pockets. To date I haven't met a single person who likes those calls, yet they are happening with greater frequency.

Right before I started writing this I got a robocall. When they call, they use a technique called "spoofing" which makes it look as though the call is coming from a number that is not the actual number. This tricks people into answering a call that may originate in another country, or even on another continent, because it appears to be from a local phone prefix. Pretty sneaky. And it must work to an acceptable extent because they are pretty common throughout the day.

My robocaller this morning spoofed a number in my phone's contact list. I was getting a call from myself!

The enemy does the same thing. He makes a call that is filled with lies and nonsense, all the while posing as someone that I should trust. Sadly, it is often easier to hang up on the robot than it is on that old liar.

Tomorrow is Election Day, so a lot of the robocalls will end, but that other nameless guy doesn't care about the calendar as much as he cares about robbing my soul. So today I will watch the incoming call numbers, tomorrow I will vote, and every day I will...

--Rise Up!!

================================

"'Watch out for false prophets. They come to you in sheep's clothing, but inwardly they are ferocious wolves.'"

-Matthew 7:15

Meditation thoughts:
Can you differentiate "real" calls from fake calls?

Who are the people in your past who are trying to spoof you?

Who are the people still in your life trying to spoof you?

Prayer:

"Dear Jesus, thank you for giving me discernment in my life. I ask you to protect me from the wolves who would do me harm. Please show me the difference between the sheep and the wolves in my life. Give me grace as I clear the meadows. I pray this in the powerful name of Jesus, Amen."

Day 8

A New Name (5.22.2023)

Our newest grandson was born last week. As you might expect, it was a joyous occasion for all of us. It was a long (25 hour) labor, but in the end Mom and baby were both great. The only real issue around his birth was that his parents couldn't decide on a name right away, so he was just "Baby" or "Him".

In our lives we go around with names that are temporary. They are just arbitrary things that people call us because they don't know our names. It might be "Addict". It might be "Felon". It might be "Drunk". It might be "Loser". There are so many things that I have been called because people give me a name that describes something they observed about me. If they did that with my grandson it might well turn out to be "Sleep" or "Poop"!

But it's not the world that gets to name us, it's our parents. My Father calls me Blessed, Highly Favored, and Redeemed. My Father knows my name, because He gave it to me. God not only knows me, but He knows my name! And he knows yours too. So don't let people call you something other than what God calls you.

Oh, by the way, after several days they decided on Oliver. Now go out there and...

--Rise Up!!

==================================

" Now you are the body of Christ, and each one of you is a part of it."
-1 Corinthians 12:27

Meditation thoughts:

Can you differentiate "real" calls from fake calls?

Who are the people in your past who are trying to spoof you?

Who are the people still in your life trying to spoof you?

Prayer:

"Dear Jesus, thank you for giving me discernment in my life. I ask you to protect me from the wolves who would do me harm. Please show me the difference between the sheep and the wolves in my life. Give me grace as I clear the meadows. I pray this in the powerful name of Jesus, Amen."

Day 9

One more year! One more year! One more year! (2.23.2015)

So we hear the "Four more years" chant with politicians all the time. I was thinking about that as I added another candle to my own birthday count. Our regular birthdays and our recovery birthdays are just ways to keep track of the calendar. The beautiful thing is that I am made new every day. I can get a fresh start with my higher power - Jesus Christ.

"Therefore if anyone is in Christ, he is a new creature; the old things passed away; behold, new things have come" - *2 Corinthians* 5:17

This is not a call to action in terms of going out and sinning in order to receive a new blessing from God. God will refresh me each morning whether I sin or not, and it's so much better when I can live my life in such a way that I keep moving onward and upward instead of the familiar two steps forward, one step back. This is why I love my Blue Chip so much. It's the First Timer's or One Day chip and it reminds me that I am always able to start on the right path regardless of where I've been traveling. Don't let the world get you down. Don't listen to the voices that cry out to you that you have failed. Listen instead to the voice of the One who has given us new life through His unending love and grace!

--Rise Up!!

================================

"Therefore if anyone is in Christ, he is a new creature; the old things passed away; behold, new things have come"

-2 Corinthians 5:17

Meditation thoughts:
    What is the issue you are working on?
    What negative voices have you listened to in the past?
    Have you been a negative voice for someone?
    What will you do start on your new path?

Prayer:
    "Dear Jesus, you have a path for me. I know that I have gone on the wrong paths in the past and I know that the one you have for me is so much

better. Lord, sometimes I get afraid of what might lie ahead of me on the path that you have laid out. Please give me courage and protection from the enemies and pitfalls that I might face as I walk with you. I pray this in the powerful name of Jesus, Amen."

Day 10

Duds (7.6.2015)

Let me start by saying that I just L-O-V-E fireworks! I love the noise, I love the flashing light, I love the colors, I love everything about fireworks... Perhaps that's not quite accurate: I'm not really that fond of the duds. I mean come on man! I paid good money, so do your thing!

Hold on there Sparky...maybe I'm racing to judgement here. Every time we have a dud it does give us the chance to let our hearts pound as we approach that firework. Perhaps we can see a faint glow of a fuse down deep inside. Perhaps not. Do I see smoke? Then as we cautiously walk toward it the stories of past mayhem go racing through our minds. Remember that guy with one eye who had one go off (my daughter's co-worker in Hawaii)? How bad will this hurt if it all goes wrong? A whole lot of risk/reward analysis happens in a short walk.

Maybe I'm wrong. Maybe I do love the duds too. After all, I could be seen as a dud. God lit my fuse long ago and I had all sorts of promise. Then after a long, slow burn I seemed to fizzle out. Heck, the world even tried to pour water on me to douse that fire. And while it succeeded on the outside, deep inside God still burned in my heart.

When we are dripping wet from the doubt of the world, God's fire is still blazing on the inside. God Made us to explode and delight. God made us to amaze people with what we could do.

It's Independence Day, light your fuse and…

--Rise Up!!

================================

"I praise you because I am fearfully and wonderfully made; your works are wonderful, I know that full well…all the days ordained for me were written in your book before one of them came to be."

-Psalms 139:14,16b

Meditation thoughts:
    Do you see yourself as a dud?
    Has God re-lit your fuse?
    What will you do to amaze people?

Prayer:

"Dear Jesus, I am a firework! As many times as you have to light my fuse, please give me the grace to keep following your lead. Do not allow me to fizzle out or be tossed to the side. I know that you have made me for a purpose; let me fulfill that. I pray this in the powerful name of Jesus, Amen."

Day 11

Swim Cap (9.8.2015)

I saw a great picture this weekend on FaceBook: there was a guy sitting near the pool wearing a swim cap. This was not a person that I would have expected to wear a swim cap, so it really amused me. The funny thing was that he had a pretty good beard going, so any aquadynamic advantage earned by wearing the cap would be severely hampered by the facial hair! I subsequently learned that he didn't even get in the pool. Perhaps it was one of those "ironic hipster" moves that millennials understand, but leave an old fogy such as myself in the dark...

It got me thinking though. How often do I do something just to make a statement? How often am I prepared for something, but unwilling to take the plunge and do it? Don't get me wrong here, I'm all for preparation and being ready for contingencies. My saddle bag on my mountain bike is basically filled with every tool I've ever needed but didn't have out on the trail. However, wearing a backpack filled with camping gear just in case I go hiking is not the wisest plan for my daily life!

As I was driving down the highway on yesterday's long-weekend drive home day, I watched carefully in case someone decided to pass while I was occupying the lane. It's just good, safe, defensive driving technique. In my recovery I try to look at what things may arise and have some kind of vague action plan to deal with life as it happens. Through prayer and meditation I am able to feel prepared. By using my sponsor, accountability partners, and Forever Family as sounding boards I am able to keep myself grounded in the midst of my daily struggles.
So here's to you Swim Cap Guy, good job being ironically prepared. Now it's time to jump in, the water's fine!

--Rise Up!!

==============================

"But in your hearts revere Christ as Lord. Always be prepared to give an answer to everyone who asks you to give the reason for the hope that you have. But do this with gentleness and respect."

-1 Peter 3:15

Meditation thoughts:

Are you a hipster or a swimmer?

Are you driving defensively in your life?

Do you have a support system to help you stay grounded? (Who is in that group?)

Am I being authentic in my walk?

Prayer:

"Dear Jesus, take the wheel! On my own, I am not equipped to face everything that this world has. Show me the places in my life where I am putting on masks. Guide me to be a positive example of your love and healing power in my life. I pray this in the powerful name of Jesus, Amen."

Day 12

The Bends (10.19.2015)

Wow! Last night I finally got the opportunity to see a recital at the Walt Disney Concert Hall at the Music Center in Los Angeles. I have been outside of this stunning building many times in the past and have been amazed at the architecture that features whimsical walls of curved sheets of stainless steel.

The walls do not follow straight lines or conform to what we see as "normal" construction. It plays with your eyes, mind, and imagination. Yet as fantastical as the outside is, the inside takes the themes and reproduces them in stunning wood, complete with curved panels. The ultimate punctuation is the massive pipe organ that occupies the far end of the hall.

So bring it around to recovery now, Paul. No problem. We are all complex individuals. The entire concept of "normal" is a farce that someone must have once proposed and somehow got people to buy-in to. There are very few straight lines in my life. As I drove home last night and reflected on the magnificent edifice that I had just been to I couldn't help but think that one of the most often used phrases that the designer heard was "It can't be done" or "that will never work". People have certainly thought and said such things about me and my recovery. How often do we get labeled as "too broken to fix" or "beyond the reach of forgiveness"? If architect Frank Gehry had listened to the doubters we would never have this visual spectacle to enjoy. If we listen to the doubters, we might never attain a state of recovery.

So what is the take away from all of this? Go with your bends. Just because it hasn't been done before doesn't mean that it can't be done. You are an original work of art, created by the Master. Let the world see and enjoy you in all your resplendent glory!

--Rise Up!!

================================

"For we are God's handiwork, created in Christ Jesus to do good works, which God prepared in advance for us to do."

-Ephesians 2:10

Meditation thoughts:

What part of me amazes people?

How have people tried to hide your masterpiece status?

How have you tried to hide your masterpiece status?

Prayer:

"Dear Jesus, you don't make mistakes and you don't make junk. I believe that I am a masterpiece. Please help me to do the things that you made me to do. When I get timid, give me boldness. Drown out the noise from my doubters. I pray this in the powerful name of Jesus, Amen."

Day 13

Overtime! (1.25.2016)

This week was a big football weekend here in the States as the two finalists for the Super Bowl were decided. A large portion of my circle of friends are fans of the Denver Broncos, so I was cheering by association with them. But if you really know me, you know that hockey is my game, so I recorded the Kings vs. Sharks game and watched it last night when I got home from a meeting for church.

I realize that many of you may not be hockey fans (I forgive you and it's not too late). Let me just let you know that this is a big rivalry game. We are the team they love to hate and vice-versa. You can probably imagine my dismay as I watched the clock dwindle down from 10 minutes to 9 to 8...still one goal behind. Then there's the moment when it goes under a minute and the clocks go super fast...ugh.

Then my miracle happened and we scored with 13 seconds left and sent the game into overtime! There I was doing a silent Snoopy dance in my living room so that I didn't wake my wife. I - WAS - HAPPY!!!

Overtime was our chance at redemption - a fresh start and we were gonna take it!

That's the way my recovery works too. I've made a lot of mistakes in my life. I've let in some goals that shouldn't have happened and I've watched people skate past me as I lay on the ice. But Jesus is my overtime. Jesus scores the tying goal for me every time I need it and He'll do it for you too.

--Rise Up!!

================================

"Christ redeemed us from the curse of the law by becoming a curse for us, for it is written: 'Cursed is everyone who is hung on a pole.' He redeemed us in order that the blessing given to Abraham might come to the Gentiles through Christ Jesus, so that by faith we might receive the promise of the Spirit."
-Galatians 3:13-14

Meditation thoughts:
When time is running out do you have hope for overtime?

What do you do as you see the clock winding down?

What did Christ save you from?

Prayer:

"Dear Jesus, when I want to give up please keep my eyes focused on you. When things seem hopeless or in doubt, please remind me that you are fighting for me. I need you in my life, Lord. I cannot do this on my own. I pray this in the powerful name of Jesus, Amen."

Day 14

The Pits (3.29.2016)

I apologize for being a day late. If it helps at all, I'm also at least a dollar short! After a busy Easter week Pastor gave us the day off yesterday so I went hiking with the grandsons. That still didn't keep me from thinking though...

Have you ever had a peach? I just LOVE peaches. Peach pie, peach cobbler, plain ol' peach...they're all great in my book. I was thinking about peaches on Friday night. Mmmmm, so tasty, just eat it and toss the pit in the trash.

Just like us....

Sometimes the world eats the peach that surrounds me then tosses the pit away. The sweet and juicy part is what the world looks forward to. The guy who will throw out rational thought. The one who will stick around for "just one more". The person who put morals aside to kick up their heels and have some fun. Yeah, the world just LOVES that guy. But the pit? Not so much. When the fun is over, when the good times go away, when the adrenaline subsides we get discarded.

But the pit is where the next peach comes from. Think about it, if we just ate all the peaches in the world but never planted that pit, we'd never get another peach. In a lot of ways, the pit is the best part of the peach. In the same ways, those of us who are in recovery are the best part of the world too. Without us to show and share the ways that we've fallen only to have God pick us back up, there might be no hope for the ones who follow behind us. And the cool thing is that there are only two kind of people in the world: those in recovery and those in denial. So get out of the pits and...

--Rise Up!!

=================================

"For what is our lot from God above, our heritage from the Almighty on high?"
-Job 31:2

Meditation thoughts:
    What is a recent peach in your life?
    What is a recent pit in your life?

Are you more about baking peach pies or planting peach trees?

Prayer:

"Dear Jesus, what an amazing world you have created for us! You have made things with such incredible detail. Make me aware of the growth that comes from pits in my life. Please remind me that everything has purpose and that one thing feeds another in your great plan. I pray this in the powerful name of Jesus, Amen."

Day 15

Family… (8.25.2016)

This has been an interesting week. I got a surprise visit from my daughter in Portland. Because of the visit I found myself taking an unexpected trip to the airport on Sunday. I made the decision to invite my Mom to spend a little time with her first grandchild and to give me a little company. This was not my first bad decision nor will it likely be my last, but it certainly played out as a bad decision.

We do not get to choose our family. We are simply there with the family we have. My trip home with my mom quickly devolved into an exercise in patience and pain. After accusing the gas station attendant of cheating her (incorrectly) I told her that it would be better to treat people with a bit more respect. This was not a popular idea. She eventually started cussing at me, calling me names, and finally declared that if I were to die, she would not miss me. This was a thought that she reiterated two more times. I have heard her say some pretty inappropriate things in my life, but this one was so shocking I just stopped talking.

Then I flew to Nashville to see my mother in law Betty

Betty is the part of my family that I chose. She belongs to a group I call my Forever Family. When I saw her, she used her entire 4 foot 10 inch frame to hug me tight. I am fixing to take a cross country road trip with her and I can't wait. I adore this lady beyond the scope of words. She is among my most favorite people in the world.

In recovery we have a forever family. This family that we choose is a group that just loves us because we are us. They do not put prerequisites on love, they simply love. They do not use our past as a weapon, they use our future for encouragement. I would not be where I am today without my Forever Family.

I still love my natural family. Regardless of the things they do and the way they treat me, I will always love them. It's because of the genetic information we share. But that Forever Family is there because of my own choice.

Find the people who love you; not the you they wish for, but the actual you that you are. That's your Forever Family. If you know them already, you are blessed. If you do not, we've got a group for that! I hope to see you soon on a Friday night.

--Rise Up!!

================================

"He replied to him, 'Who is my mother, and who are my brothers?' Pointing to his disciples, he said, 'Here are my mother and my brothers. For whoever does the will of my Father in heaven is my brother and sister and mother.'"

-Matthew 12:48-50

Meditation thoughts:
What difficult relationships do I have with my biological family?
Who have I added to my Forever Family?
Who has added me to their Forever Family?

Prayer:
"Dear Jesus, thank you for my family. Thank you for putting people into my life who are there to

help me get through difficult times and to celebrate the victories with me. Lord, where I have had problems with my family, I ask you to show me the path to redemption. Please help me to keep safe boundaries in my life. I pray this in the powerful name of Jesus, Amen."

Day 16

Weebles (8.21.2017)

Anyone else remember Weebles? Yeah, they wobble but they don't fall down. I never had any, but always wanted them. I remember going into Fedco in Panorama City before Christmas back in the 70's. They had a table out with lots of toys to try out. I was DETERMINED to get a Weeble to fall down. I did everything that I could to knock that rascal down to no avail. You see Weebles were an egg shaped toy that was weighted at the bottom so they just popped upright every time. I left impressed but defeated.

The devil likes to shop at my Fedco and play with the toys. He thinks he can knock me down and keep me there, but he couldn't be "wronger"! Philippians 4:13 reminds me that I will not fail because I am on the right side of the fight. Satan WILL try. Satan WILL fail! We WILL...

--Rise Up!!

==================================

"I can do all this through him who gives me strength.."

-Philippians 4:13

Meditation thoughts:

Where do you need strength?

Are you looking to be strong or will you be weak and let God do the heavy lifting?

How does the enemy try to knock you over?

Prayer:

"Dear Jesus, I need you to be strong. I need to see that my strength alone will never be enough. When the enemy tries to push me over, I trust you to put me back upright. Thank you for loving me so much. I pray this in the powerful name of Jesus, Amen."

Day 17

Luc (12.11.2017)

I guess a post about costumes may seem about 6 weeks late to some of you, but bear with me. Last night I was FaceTiming with my grandson Luc. When his dad answered he let me know that Luc wanted to "surprise" me with his Hulk costume. Grammy and I gave the required shocked response and things were good. A bit later we noticed that Hulk Luc had disappeared. He was soon replaced by Captain America Luc. Then later the same events were repeated with the final result being Cat Boy Luc.

Every outfit he put on to try and disguise himself looked different, but the essence of who was inside remained. It was always Luc.

When we introduce ourselves at Celebrate Recovery we always start with a phrase like "I am a grateful Christian believer...". I have put on a lot of costumes over the years. I've been teacher. I've been husband. I've been inmate. All of those looked different from the outside, but I was always a grateful Christian believer underneath it all. People love labels. Check under the tree and you'll probably find a bunch of them. The label doesn't define the thing though. The way I see it, if a label is needed it probably means that someone probably wants to define something in a way that is either not obvious or often in a way that is misleading. If you need my label, I'll settle for Grateful Christian Believer. And before I wrap up, I will...

--Rise Up!!

================================

"But you are a chosen people, a royal priesthood, a holy nation, God's special possession, that you may declare the praises of him who called you out of darkness into his wonderful light."
-1 Peter 2:9

Meditation thoughts:
    Do you believe that God chose you? Why?
    What label(s) have you been given?
    What do you do to live with your past?
    What is the label that you choose for yourself?
    Do you accept other people's labels for your life or do you insist that they use your true name?

Prayer:
> "Dear Jesus, thank you for calling me out of the darkness. Me. I know that you chose me because you love me. Help me to be authentic in my walk. Let people see you in my life instead of just me. I pray this in the powerful name of Jesus, Amen."

Day 18

Two Steps Forward… (12.18.2017)

Life...am I right?!?

So often I feel like life is a continuous diet of two steps forward, one step back. That can be so frustrating. But it's still forward progress. If you watch football at all you are probably familiar with the concept of forward progress. It's where they place the ball at the most forward point that the runner reached. This is to make it so that the defender doesn't pick a person up and carry them backward. That would be cheating.

Here's a secret...the enemy is a cheater! He tries to pick me up and throw me backward all the time. But MY God is a great referee and he spots the ball at my forward progress. First Down!

So as this holiday season wears on and wears in, keep in mind that you are probably making forward progress. Every backward step is in preparation for two steps forward. Take heart, we are all doing this together. We will reach the goal because we will…

--Rise Up!!

===============================

"Trust in the Lord with all your heart and lean not on your own understanding; in all your ways submit to him, and he will make your paths straight"

-Proverbs 3:5-6

Meditation thoughts:
How has the enemy cheated you?
What do you do to recognize your progress?
How do I show trust in God?

Prayer:
"Dear Jesus, help me to make progress each day. Please shine your light in front of me so that I know where to put each step. I am asking you to help me to recognize that even when I move backward you will ensure that I go further forward than I go backward. I pray this in the powerful name of Jesus, Amen."

Day 19

I Don't Know Jesus... (1.22.2018)

Recently I was sitting in a group of men. As we introduced ourselves we started with the standard CR intro of "I'm a grateful Christian believer who struggles with..." Then one person borrowed (and slightly changed) a line from *Ghost Busters*. He said "I don't know Jesus, but I like his style." That thought has been rattling around in my head for a couple of weeks now.

The only way that people will know Jesus' style is to know something about Jesus, ergo, if they know me and I know Jesus they will get some kind of impression about Jesus through my walk. Now just because this happens does not mean that I am the best example of Jesus to be found, but that doesn't matter. People know that I am a Christian and they will naturally make assumptions about Jesus when they watch me. So what kind of Jesus am I representing? What do they think about Jesus when they see the fish on my car driving down the road? Is he a selfish rule-breaker? Does he know how to use a blinker (both on AND off!)? Does my T-Shirt with the clever pun make them want to know my savior or does my sarcasm and behavior repel them? When people look at me, will they like Jesus' style or will they want him to go away as fast as possible?

If the goal is to win people for Christ and the only thing I do is open the doors on Friday night and Sunday morning there's a really good chance that I am delusional about my walk, mission, and call. Whatever you think your calling is is up to you and God. I can't say what you were called to do, but I know clearly what we are told to do and that is to go into all the nations and bring those folks the Good News. There are plenty of folks who will bash them over the head with their stupid picket sign. Let's be the Jesus that loves people. Let's show them that we can....

--Rise Up!!

================================

"In your relationships with one another, have the same mindset as Christ Jesus"

-Philippians 2:5

Meditation thoughts:

How well do you know Jesus?
What do people think when they see you?
Does your walk match your talk?

Prayer:

"Dear Jesus, I want to be more like you. I want the people that I know to know you. Help me to share your message and love, and if necessary, give me the words to use. I pray this in the powerful name of Jesus, Amen."

Day 20

Gate Clearance (4.30.2018)

I went to prison on Saturday. I was all set to meet "the guys" doing CR there. Weeks of anticipation, no years of anticipation were about to be ended as my new journey began. I drove across the miles of empty desert and listened to worship music, trying to prepare my heart and soul for what was to come. My current "go to" worship song was playing on the radio as I parked the car. I soaked it in, said a prayer, and headed for the entrance.

When I got into the employee entrance the CO (Corrections Officer) at the desk asked me about my business there today. He took my ID and ran it through the computer. Then he just looked at me. Then he looked through the papers in front of him. Then he asked me again why I was there. We ran through this cycle several times. It was explained to me that I had gate clearance, but no escort. No one had alerted them to the fact that I would be there on that day.

Phone and radio calls were made and eventually a Lieutenant came to talk to me. We did the same dance moves from my earlier interaction with the men at the entrance desk and when the music ended we were in pretty much the same place: gate clearance and no escort.

I saw that I had a few choices. I had done everything in my power to follow protocol (including calling ahead of my visit). I had driven an hour to get there and I arrived 30 minutes early to give plenty of time and not cause stress on anyone. I wore the proper clothing. I even brought my whistle. I was squared away and then some. They were not. It was on them to fix this and not waste my time, right?!? WRONG!

The other choice that I had was to be gracious. I chose to model calm and understanding. I chose to be reasonable and let them know that what they were doing was more important than what I was doing. I let them know that I had waited for 16 years to be standing in just such a spot so one more week was not a big deal at all. I said nothing about wasted time and gas. I chose, right then and there to...

--Rise Up!!

===============================

"The Lord is compassionate and gracious, slow to anger, abounding in love."

Psalms 103:8

Meditation thoughts:

How do you handle disappointment?
What do you do when it isn't your fault?
How do you show grace?

Prayer:

"Dear Jesus, sometimes my life gets frustrating. Sometimes things happen that are out of my control. Please keep my emotions in control. Please let me experience the fruit of the spirit. Let others see me as a keeper of peace. I need your love in my life in order to show love, so please, Lord, give me an extra measure of grace today. I pray this in the powerful name of Jesus, Amen."

The Lord is compassionate and gracious, slow to anger, abounding in love.

(Psalms 103:8)

Meditation thoughts
How do you handle disappointment?
What do you do when I lead you astray?
How do you show you care?

Prayer:

"Dear Jesus, sometimes, in life's pain I lament. Sometimes things happen that are out of my control. Please keep me focused in a much as possible on the importance of the truth of the words of hope, as also hope of peace of mind, that love in my life is better to show love just, that is Lord, give me ... share message of grace today. I pray this in the mighty name of Jesus, Amen."

82

Day 21

Try (6.4.2018)

Some people try and some people do not, or at least they don't try in a way that seems obvious to the rest of us.

I went to visit my granddaughter this weekend. Because of my past, her mother is not always willing to allow visits. Over the past few weeks we have planned a family trip for her birthday. The day before the trip her mother did it again and said that I was not really welcome to join. Being that I typically do all of the driving on family trips I still decided to join. I had a cold and felt miserable. I was tired from a trip out of town two days before. I was not looking forward to spending a weekend in a hotel with no transportation, but I did it anyway. I wanted to set an example for my family, but for my son in particular, that we always do everything we can.

The first day of the trip I spent a few hours in a Starbucks while the party happened at a local park. I was completely surprised that I was allowed to then go to dinner with everyone after the party. Try.

Day two had a trip to the aquarium. Again, I was persona non grata. I spent the next six or seven hours wandering around the Cannery Row area of Monterey. I ate some saltwater taffy. I had a monstrously huge pancake. I got a surprise visit from a friend who joined me for lunch. I drank more coffee. I sat by the shore. Try.

As I sat watching the waves against the sand and rocks I noticed a plant growing in a small crevice of the seaside granite. What on earth was this doing here? How did it have the temerity to grow where there was nothing else? That's right...it tried

It was frustrating to watch my son spend time on his cell phone instead of interacting with his daughter. It was hard driving thirteen hours while sick and hearing him snore all the way there and back. Like I said, sometimes another person's efforts might not be as obvious as I'd like, but that has no real bearing on my own efforts. This weekend was a success. All I needed to do was try and…

--Rise Up!!

===============================

"Consider it pure joy, my brothers and sisters, whenever you face trials of many kinds, because you know that the testing of your faith produces perseverance. Let perseverance finish its work so that you may be mature and complete, not lacking anything."

-James 1:2-4

Meditation thoughts:
Where do you need to persevere in your life?
What can you do to help you persevere?
How can you focus on trials as joy?
How are you allowing perseverance to finish its work in your life?

Prayer:
"Dear Jesus, help me to focus my life on the good and positive things. Please give me perseverance in my trials. Please help me to see the trials as a way forward in my walk. Build my faith through these difficult times that I will face. I pray this in the powerful name of Jesus, Amen."

Day 22

Cliffs (9.17.2018)

I took a trip to South Point last week. My son in law Dave took me out so that we could see the southernmost tip of the United States. It was pretty cool. After we walked toward the ocean we turned and went up the coast a few hundred meters. Gradually the land rose and we found ourselves on a cliff about 30 feet above the ocean.

I got to thinking about how often the beauty of life can be surrounded by danger. The higher up we go, the better the view can be. Here I was surrounded by rugged land, beautiful water, gorgeous plants and flowers galore, and what was my purpose here? To jump. Are you like that too? Nothing is ever enough? Well the view from that cliff just wasn't enough to look at, so we jumped! Thirty feet of free fall was followed by a hard splash into the ocean. My arms stung a bit because I left them out when I entered. Now the rush of the jump was gone and all I could think was "Shark!". I had no reason to think this other than paranoia built out of a lifetime living with Jaws in the back of my mind. So I swam like crazy to get to the ladder.

Here was my source of rescue - a rusty ladder, the rungs wrapped in duct tape, hanging from two bolts at the top of the cliff. The bolts made it swing in and out with the waves. It didn't look safe, and I wasn't sure that I wanted to be on it, but I did know that I wanted to get out of that water.

I guess what I'm trying to say is that sometimes I do things that seem like a good idea. Sometimes I go places that look pleasing but turn out scary. Sometimes the way out of danger doesn't seem like fun. But that ladder was like my recovery, I had to work hard and it was uncomfortable and even a bit scary, but it let me...

--Rise Up!!

================================

"For the Lord your God is the one who goes with you to fight for you against your enemies to give you victory."

-Deuteronomy 20:4

Meditation thoughts:

What is providing your safety route?
What challenge are you facing right now?
How will you overcome this challenge?

Prayer:

"Dear Jesus, thank you for being my ladder to safety. Thank you for rescuing me from the waves and bringing me back to shore. Thank you for calming the storms. Lord, I know that I can do anything with your help, so please keep me moving past pride and fear so that I can be successful with you. I pray this in the powerful name of Jesus, Amen."

Day 23

Happy Accidents (5.20.2019)

I got together with my podcasting co-host yesterday. As is our routine, we did not come into the show with anything other than the most basic outline for the show. By that I mean we had a Word of the Week and a Song of the Week ready. We also thought about one or two topics that we could discuss, but nothing specific and certainly nothing more than just that.

As we talked God took over. Somehow, and neither of us could remember how it happened, we began talking about a painful issue in both of our former lives. The conversation became deep and rich. Here's my brief point. It's not a bad idea to plan things out (I love order), but don't forget to leave room for God in those plans. He always shows up, and He always has something wonderful for us. Next time you wonder "Is it odd, or is it God?" go with the second option. He's helping you to…

--Rise Up!!

=================================

"For those who are led by the Spirit of God are the children of God."

-Romans 8:14

Meditation thoughts:
   Am I open to being led by the Spirit?
   How do I respond to the Spirit in my life?
   Have I had an opportunity to ask "Is it odd or is it God"?

Prayer:
   "Dear Jesus, thank you for the gift of the Holy Spirit in my life. I am so thankful that I don't have to make my own way, but that I can lean on you to guide my steps. Please pour your Spirit out to me today. I pray this in the powerful name of Jesus, Amen."

Day 24

Well Dang! (5.18.2020)

You can file this under best laid plans of mice and men...

On our trip across this beautiful land yesterday we encountered some snags. Go figure! We had taken a side trip to visit "Carhenge" (read more about it at paulpippen.com/blog) which was awesome. We then proceeded to drive through the Nebraska and Wyoming night toward our final destination of Casper, Wyoming. Everything seemed copacetic until we got about 8 miles outside of the hamlet of Lusk, then it all went off the rails.

I suppose off the pavement is more precise. There was road construction and it began, as it usually does, with a sign announcing said construction. No problem, we've been seeing this a bunch on our trip. It's actually a great idea to fix the roads while the traffic is so light. Bravo, Department of Transportation! However, even though the "Road Work Ahead" was accurate, the "Grooves in Pavement" sign was a straight up lie! The pavement was gone. We drove over 5 miles on a dirt bed that came factory equipped with huge holes, nasty ruts, and occasionally a massive ridge in the center of the lane. I winced as I heard the bottom of the car scrape that ridge several times. It was all unavoidable.

So is life. And recovery. Sometimes you are cruising along wonderfully and then life throws you a curve. Life tends to not stick to the script. It likes to ad lib. Life thinks it's a comedian, but oftentimes, I don't get the joke.

That's ok. Actually, that's life! I try to enjoy those quirks and foibles and find some benefit or lesson from it all. Yeah, it's bumpy at times, but it's also beautiful.

Keep your wheels on the road and continue to...

--Rise Up!!

================================

"Blessed are those whose ways are blameless, who walk according to the law of the Lord…
I will praise you with an upright heart as I learn your righteous laws. I will obey your decrees;"
-Psalms 119:1,7 & 8a

Meditation thoughts:

What do I do when the pavement turns to dirt?

When I hit bumps and holes, what is my response?

Do I keep moving forward long enough to reach the destination and safety?

Prayer:

"Dear Jesus, your roads are always the best. When I find myself in trouble, please help me to remember your will for me. Please help me to remember that out of everyone on Earth, that I am your favorite. Keep me moving past the bumps. I pray this in the powerful name of Jesus, Amen."

Day 25

Snap (6.15.2020)

My grandson recently discovered Snap Chat. He's 5. They have crazy effects. That should tell you most of what you need to know!

He loves to make funny faces and send them to Papa, because "Papa is funny". It's good to have a "thing" and with Luc, my "thing" is being funny. Now he wants to be "funny like Papa".

We are all emulating something or someone at a certain point. We try to follow in someone's footsteps. For Luc, he's trying to follow in mine. What he doesn't realize is that I am trying to follow someone else, which means that there are far more feet than just mine and his in those footprints.

My question is whose feet are you following and who is following yours? These are important questions as we make our way through life. We need to be sure that their feet and our feet are worthy.

It's like having and being a sponsor in recovery. Before someone chooses a sponsor they should watch and observe to be certain that the walk matches the talk. We also need to see if those footprints will lead us too close to the cliffs in life. The distance from an amazing view and a horrible accident are often just a few steps.

That's it for this week. Enjoy your walk, and...

--Rise Up!!

================================

"Whoever claims to live in him must live as Jesus did."

-1 John 2:6

Meditation thoughts:
Who has guided you up to this point in your life?
Are you acting as a guide for anyone?
Is it time for you to reconsider who influences you?

Prayer:
"Dear Jesus, my steps are so important to me. I pray that you will clear the rocks from my path so that I can walk with assurance. Lord, when people look to me as an example, please help me to shine with your light and not my own. Let my

example be for your glory. I pray this in the powerful name of Jesus, Amen."

Day 26

Let Your Light Shine (12.7.2020)

I took my Mom to a follow-up appointment with her hip surgeon on Thursday. It was meant to be a relatively short trip with a stop for lunch and Costco added into the mix. Leave at 11, home in time for a Zoom conference call at 6. Easy peasy.

That should give you most of the information you need to finish the story...

Everything was great up to and through our lunch. We had to eat in the car because of new COVID guidelines, but it was all very pleasant. After a quick side trip to Krispy Kreme we started our journey home by pointing the car toward Costco.

When we hit the front door at Costco, the ball of yarn began to unravel.

The first signal of impending doom was that Mom stopped right inside the door to fish out her list and to put away her card. I gently (honestly!) suggested that she move out of the flow of traffic to do all this, and after a small amount of cajoling, she did. Good job, on with the shopping!

The theme of the afternoon quickly became me trying to get her to not walk down the middle of the aisles. I tried to point out that she was slow (just a couple weeks on that shiny new hip after all) and that it made for a better shopping experience for all of us if she tried to stay close to one side or the other. She did not seem to agree and kept drifting to the center.

Eventually I decided that it would be a good idea if I put her and her cart in one spot and brought her desired items back to her. I am far more mobile and this method would certainly get us out of there faster. I had plenty of time built into the schedule, but I didn't want to have to try to be on a conference call and drive that evening. It worked sufficiently in the fruit and produce area, but when we needed to move to other parts of the store, this plan was not as workable.

[Cut to an old woman wandering the center aisle of Costco with younger people patiently stacking up behind her.]

Our next item was yogurt. She insisted, I mean really, really, really insisted that it was in the closest cold aisle to us. I pointed out that the two big boxes making the aisle were both freezers and therefore would not have yogurt in them. She let me know, in no uncertain terms, that she KNEW where yogurt was. I offered to place $1000 on each of our theories. She did not find the humor in my suggestion and instead asked an employee. He told her the same information I gave her, which to her ears sounded better. Yogurt was, indeed, in the refrigerator, not the freezer.

[Cut to Paul getting more cranky.]

The rest of the shopping devolved into more of the same- me trying to get an 86 year old lady to change the way she's always done things. One of my favorite "Recoveryisms" is ""Expectations are premeditated resentments." I should have known better.

Eventually I took a photo of her in the aisle to try and demonstrate to her that she really was blocking traffic. She got mad and told me that "if they want to get by, they can honk." That was my final straw. I put the box of Clif Bars I was holding into the cart and told her I was done and I'd see her at the front of the store.

Wait a minute, that's not exactly right, is it? Sure, I put that box in the cart, but it certainly wasn't a Step 5 "exact nature of our wrongs" kind of telling of the story. I chucked them in there with a bit of pep. It was ridiculous and I'm sure people thought things of me that weren't really kind.

Now I'm standing on the other side of the checkout counters fuming. No, pouting. Well, I suppose I was doing quite a lot of both!

Now for the fun part...

As I'm leaning against the wall and stewing I see an employee walk by. As he does, he gives an encouraging word to a fellow employee. "Let your light shine..."

Ughhhhh. Jesus smacked me right in the kisser with that one. I knew what the guy meant. Now mind you, he had no idea what had transpired, none whatsoever. He was just telling his mate to be a good person and not let the chaos get to them.

I spent the rest of the trip in silent reflection. Not one word on a 90 minute drive. I definitely knew what I needed to do, but couldn't muster the gumption. I was ignoring the "prompt" part of Step 10. I left things foul that night when I dropped Mom off, but the Spirit kept working on me all night.

The next day I drove to Mom's house and gave her a hug and a kiss. I told her that I loved her and that I behaved poorly. I told her that I was wrong.

That's the job, people. I can never stop working my steps. How could I go up and teach a lesson on amends but be unwilling to do it in my own life?

It's always best to be prompt, but however long it takes, we can always...

--Rise Up!!

================================

"In the same way, let your light shine before others, that they may see your good deeds and glorify your Father in heaven."

-Matthew 5:16

Meditation thoughts:

When was the last time you put a lampshade over your lamp?

Are you able to recognize your mistakes in the moment?

How do you seek forgiveness and amends?

Do you owe someone amends? If so, what is keeping you from acting?

Prayer:

"Dear Jesus, forgive me where I have covered your light with my own selfish behavior. Lord, I ask you right now, in this moment, to heal my selfish spirit. Please give me wisdom and grace as I make amends with the people I have hurt. I pray this in the powerful name of Jesus, Amen."

Day 27

5 New Faces (11.8.2021)

Friday was one of those days that I don't necessarily relish. I could see in advance that things were not going to be pleasant for a bit. I even knew in advance and agreed to set some of the conditions that allowed for the unpleasantness. Yet still, with all this "foreknowledge", I stormed into the rain and complained about getting wet.

One of the biggest tenets of recovery is that consistency in your program is critical. People are often unstable and they need to be able to predict what is coming next. Changes in routines are going to happen, but we like to try to minimize their frequency. Through "circumstances beyond our control" we were moved into a different venue for our group on Friday. There was a scheduling conflict and we were asked to accommodate a change. I wasn't pleased, but these things happen, right? I agreed to the change days in advance, but as the calendar drew us closer to Friday I got more and more bothered about my decision. I let myself hear that my group was "less than"; that we were once again seen as "those people".

As I drove up early on Friday afternoon to try to move and set up equipment I discovered that I was woefully under equipped to do things in a way that we had become used to doing them. Cue the angry voices and accusations in my mind. Galatians 5:22 & 23 tell us about the fruit of the spirit. It's fairly well known in Christian circles. The lead in verses (19-21) tell us about the works of the flesh. Nestled in there amongst the foul and filth is "fits of anger". Yeah, that was me late Friday afternoon.

I'd love to tell you that I realized my mistake and got over myself quickly, but that's just not the way it played out. I pouted and fumed. I figuratively stamped my feet and pounded my fists. I wanted to quit. I wanted to light a match and burn it all down. Not a particularly great look for the Ministry Leader of a recovery program...

We did not have the requisite equipment to do an electric worship service so we opted for an acoustic set. We went unplugged, including no microphones. That meant we had to sing loud in order to be heard well. Sing loud...now that sounded like something I was up for! We practiced our worship set and I began to calm down. I let God soothe me through the worship. I let myself laugh. Then God happened...

On a night where we were not in our normal venue; on a night when the church campus had dozens of people coming for a completely different event; on a night where it was all supposed to go wrong we had our biggest attendance in months including 5 brand new faces and 2 others who were there for the other event, but committed to returning next week for CR. God is so good. Just when I was reaching for the depths He showed me how to...

--Rise Up!!

================================

"The acts of the flesh are obvious: sexual immorality, impurity and debauchery; idolatry and witchcraft; hatred, discord, jealousy, fits of rage, selfish ambition, dissensions, factions and envy; drunkenness, orgies, and the like. I warn you, as I did before, that those who live like this will not inherit the kingdom of God.

But the fruit of the Spirit is love, joy, peace, forbearance, kindness, goodness, faithfulness, gentleness and self-control. Against such things there is no law."

-Galatians 5:19-23

Meditation thoughts:

What does it look like when you go into an obvious storm?

What is a time where you got an unexpected blessing?

Do you have fruit salad or just one big fruit of the spirit?

Prayer:

"Dear Jesus, your blessings are new everyday, but sometimes I don't want to see that. Thank you for helping me move through my disappointments and anger in order to enjoy blessings. Lord, please keep me hungry for more of your fruit. I pray this in the powerful name of Jesus, Amen."

Day 28

Magic (3.14.2022)

I used to love roller coasters. I could ride all day, do the loops, and have no problems. I was never really great with spinning, but loops and coasters were my jam.
Then I got older.
Now, one spin, one loop, one corkscrew and I'm out of commission for the rest of the day. It's sad to me because I loved riding roller coasters so much. So when my grandson invited us to go to Magic Mountain for his 13th birthday I said yes, but told him that my favorite ride was gonna be the bench!
I waited in line with them. I watched the cars go careening around the twisted steel and felt that old rush of adrenaline. I wanted to ride, but I knew my limits. They tried to convince me it would be ok. They tried to tell me how it really wasn't that bad. But I knew better and said no.
But the cool thing about amusement parks is that they have some rides that are decidedly more tame. Even a place like Magic Mountain that boasts 20 thrill rides has a few things that your MoM can

handle. My boys love me enough that they sacrificed part of their fun so that I could ride some of the smaller, older coasters. No loops. No big vortexes. Just good old fashioned hills and thrills.

In the end I was able to go on three rides: two old coasters and a flume ride. It wasn't the world's most dangerous outing, but it still gave me a chance to...

--Rise Up!!

=================================

"That is why, for Christ's sake, I delight in weaknesses, in insults, in hardships, in persecutions, in difficulties. For when I am weak, then I am strong."

-2 Corinthians 12:10

Meditation thoughts:
    How has your walk changed as you age?
    How do you recognize your limitations?
    How do you accept your limitations?

Prayer:

"Dear Jesus, I know that I cannot do the things that I used to be able to do. I know that I am changing as I grow in You. Please help me to see these changes as something to embrace rather than something to resent. I pray this in the powerful name of Jesus, Amen."

Day 29

Ruined? (3.21.2022)

Friday is my day for Celebrate Recovery. There's a fair amount of set up and clean up to do before and after our meetings. In order to make our night a bit shorter I took an opportunity to do some clean up while the ladies were still having their open share group. I put away the food and tables. I reset the chairs. I turned off the sound equipment. I left the coffee on...
Ooops!
Yup, me, the Minister of Mocha, your MoM, forgot to turn off the coffee machine and left the pot on the burner. 24 hours later I was sitting in San Diego at a Seals lacrosse game and got a phone call from our pastor. He let me know that someone had come in and found the pot smoking on the burner. Uggh. The pot was ruined. Bigger uggh.
Now I had a choice. As the leader it would be easy to shirk the responsibility and let him think that it was someone else who had made the mistake, you know, shrug at the uggh. Instead I fessed up to him then made a call to the person who runs the coffee

ministry at the church to let them know that it was me that made the mistake and that I would replace the pot that had been ruined. The phone call took her by surprise. She was thankful for my honesty. Since so many different ministries use the coffee station, she gets a lot of shoulder shrugs when things go wrong. Somebody else must have done it is a typical response.

After I confessed and a strange thing happened: nothing. Confessing can feel scary, but it usually is not a problem. It's just putting Step 10 into action. We recognize when we make a mistake, then we address it promptly. It's really OK.

Next time you have a fall, break out Step 10 and...

--Rise Up!!

================================

"Then he said to them all: 'Whoever wants to be my disciple must deny themselves and take up their cross daily and follow me.'"

-Luke 9:23

Meditation thoughts:

How do you acknowledge your blunders?

Are there areas where you are maintaining lies and denial?

What would happen if you were to admit your latest failure?

Prayer:

"Dear Jesus, you picked up a cross for me. Please give me the courage to bear my own cross. Yet I know that if I lean on you, I can enjoy the light yoke because you bear the heavy weight for me. Help me to admit when I am wrong and help me to do so quickly. I pray this in the powerful name of Jesus, Amen."

118

Day 30

The New New (11.28.2022)

I never write these things until I write them. What I mean by that is that I try not to think about the blog until I'm writing it. I don't have a file of "good blog topics" on my computer. I want it to be whatever occurs to me at the moment. Thursday I had some things pop up in life that seemed like possible candidates. Then Friday I had some that were even better. As I sat in my local Starbucks this morning I thought I had a good idea to write on, then I got a text from my daughter who lives in Hawaii that Mauna Loa was erupting. Talk about "the floor is lava"!

Lava and volcanoes really don't have a lot to do with recovery. I could talk about lava being fresh rock and how we always get a fresh start with Jesus. I could talk about lava spewing into the sky and have a really good on-ramp to my "Rise Up" ending. I could talk about the destruction of an eruption eventually being the creation of something beautiful. Without giving away too many of my "trade secrets" for writing, there are lots of avenues to explore with the volcano.

The thing that stands out though is that life is constantly evolving. Stasis is fickle at best. Even when you think you've got a plan, things can change. As Mike Tyson famously said, "Everyone has a plan until they get punched in the face." So enjoy your day, avoid the lava, recognize that you might be witnessing the creation of something beautiful, and...

--Rise Up!!

================================

"Put to death, therefore, whatever belongs to your earthly nature…you have taken off your old self with its practices and have put on the new self, which is being renewed in knowledge in the image of its Creator."

-Colossians 3:5,9b-10

Meditation thoughts:
    Do you have a plan?
    What happens when you get punched in the face?

What will you look like when the next change is done?

Prayer:

"Dear Jesus, I need a plan in my life. For too long I have tried to do it on my own with my plan. Reveal your plan to me. Help me to put off my own ideas so that I can embrace yours. I pray this in the powerful name of Jesus, Amen."

Day 31

Going Out (1.16.2023)

This morning I was awakened by a tiny kiss on the cheek. I'm visiting my grandkids and that's how it goes in the morning: little patter of little 3 year old ("Going on Four, Papa") feet then a kiss on the cheek. It's the best!

Today we had planned on going out to breakfast as a fam. As I sit downstairs I can hear protests from the same sweet lips that so recently kissed my cheek. "I don't wanna go, Mommmmmmmmmmy!"

Wow, that's my recovery right there. Stuff I need to do, but just don't want to. I'm happy one minute, then wailing and sobbing the next. Now my daughter has calmed her down. She's like my sponsor. She just listened then helped her figure out the problems. Now we're good to go. Everything is set for us to…

--Rise Up!!

=================================

"I do not understand what I do. For what I want to do I do not do, but what I hate I do."
-*Romans 7:15*

Meditation thoughts:

What do you look forward to?

Do your wishes bring pain or problems for the other people in your life?

Are you doing what you want to do or what you should do?

Prayer:

"Dear Jesus, please guide every step in my life. When I see things that I need to change, please help bend me to your way. When people try to help me, please help me to listen. I pray this in the powerful name of Jesus, Amen."

Day 32

Healing and Forgiveness (5.29.2023)

I suppose what I really mean is that healing is forgiveness. The past week I was in the prison with the fellas and we were discussing the idea of God healing us physically. The question was posed "Does God still heal people?" After much discussion we heard a story of a man who struggled with renal failure. He had a kidney transplant, but it was not successful and he spent the next 25 years going to dialysis treatments every week. The man's perspective was that God healed him by giving him eternal security, but that he was still allowed to suffer here on earth.

One of our students was moved by this story and perspective. He is back inside serving another long term. During previous stretches he has lost family members, including his mother. Before this current sentence his father told him that he needed to stay out of prison because he didn't think he would live long enough to see his son come back home. That projection has been found to be true. The man in our class talked about how he had seen so many "good

Christian people" in his life not get saved from health issues long enough for him to have a reunion after a particular release. This drove a wedge between him and God. He was angry with God for taking these people that he saw as righteous, while leaving him here in his criminal thinking and sin.

With tears in his eyes and in his voice he spoke about a freedom that he was receiving after being able to change his perspective on what healing really was. The other men in class also had tears in their eyes as they listened to him pour out his heart.

We've all carried around burdens that we thought we had to bear. Hopefully we have also come to the understanding that we serve a loving God who has our best interests at heart. For my student, it took a story and a shift of perspective to get him to let go of his weight. What will it take for you to let go and..

--Rise Up!!

=================================

"Do not conform to the pattern of this world, but be transformed by the renewing of your mind. Then you will be able to test and approve what God's will is—his good, pleasing and perfect will."

-Romans 12:2

Meditation thoughts:

What healing are you waiting for?
What miracles have you seen in your life?
Do you need to change your definitions of healing?

Prayer:

"Dear Jesus, thank you for bringing healing into my life. Lord, I need your healing in my life. Release my mind from my own thinking and help me to see the miracles you provide. I am asking you for patience in waiting on your answers. I pray this in the powerful name of Jesus, Amen."

Day 33

Jackhammer (4.12.2021)

Today is my first Monday back after 5 beautiful weeks in Hawaii. That's not to say that Ridgecrest isn't beautiful, it's just not Hawaii beautiful. Today in Ridgecrest just happened to be gorgeous. Most spring days are.

My plan today was to take my friend over to a house and bust out a concrete slab for another friend. They were supplying me with a jackhammer, I had a helper, and it was only about 2 yards of concrete to bust out. I did the thing you never do: I told my helper that this would be easy. "We're going to be out of here by 10." Right now it's 5pm and I'm in the shower dictating this post to my wife so I can get ready in time for my 6:00 step study. So much for easy!

Everything started out fine but about 10 minutes into the job the jackhammer decided it was time for a break. It became as fickle as a kid in a candy store; it didn't know what it wanted and it couldn't decide what to do. This job is a Step 12 "giving back" kind of job. No money is being exchanged, it's just me trying to give back.

As I worked I remembered I hadn't written the blog. I kept thinking to myself "You better find a way to rise up". Eventually with the help of my brand new sledgehammer and pick ax, a helpful visit from my two oldest grandsons, and a whole lot of hard work we got done.

It would have been much easier to walk away. After all, this was not a paying job so I wouldn't lose out on a paycheck. But that's not what Step 12 is about and that's not what recovery's about. We're giving back not taking off.

My hands are sore. My feet are sore. I have several blisters that I didn't have this morning. I'm worn out and exhausted. But boy oh boy, did I ever...

--Rise Up!!

================================

"Anyone who has been stealing must steal no longer, but must work, doing something useful with their own hands, that they may have something to share with those in need."

-Ephesians 4:28

Meditation thoughts:

What are some gifts that I could share?
Where could I give back?
Am I waiting for someone to ask me to help or am I seeking areas to be of service?

Prayer:

"Dear Jesus, use me. You have given me skills and talents so that I can help others. Please show me areas where I can be of service. Please give me a willing heart. Thank you for bringing me to a place in my walk where I can see my own value. Please give me boldness in my walk. I pray this in the powerful name of Jesus, Amen."

Day 34

Gone Missing (9.16.2019)

I was recently volunteering at a local prison when they lost track of an inmate. Initially they sent guards around to check in classes to see if the inmate was talking to a teacher. It seems that the search turned out to be fruitless. An hour later another guard came in and told everyone to go back to their cells for an emergency count. That signaled the end of my work day, so I went home.

Jesus does that same thing for us. When we go missing, most people won't notice or even care. Not Jesus. He cares. He will search room to room for us. He will shut down the whole operation just to find the one lost sheep. As you go out there to face a new day and a new week, remember that you are loved by Jesus and...

--Rise Up!!

================================

"'Suppose one of you has a hundred sheep and loses one of them. Doesn't he leave the ninety-nine in the open country and go after the lost sheep until he finds it? And when he finds it, he joyfully puts it on his shoulders and goes home. Then he calls his friends and neighbors together and says, "Rejoice with me; I have found my lost sheep." I tell you that in the same way there will be more rejoicing in heaven over one sinner who repents than over ninety-nine righteous persons who do not need to repent.'"

-Luke 15:4-7

Meditation thoughts:

When have I been the one sheep that went missing?

When Jesus looked for me did I run to him or hide even deeper?

What did I do when I was brought back into the fold?

Prayer:

"Dear Jesus, thank you for looking for me. I know that I have wandered in the past, but I ask you to help keep me in the safety of your flock. Thank you for loving me so much that you will make me your priority. Give me the assurance that you will always search for me, even if I wander again. I pray this in the powerful name of Jesus, Amen."

Day 35

Cheeks (12.9.2024)

Sometimes our past behavior gets brought back into life. People find it lying on the side of the road and try to re-enact the whole Good Samaritan routine on its lifeless body. A little CPR, a little rescue breathing, maybe even slapping some paddles on it..."Clear!"...anything to help people remember who we used to be. Instead of normal life saving techniques, the modern method usually involves social media blasts.

Here's my advice on this type of thing. I speak from experience, so indulge me if you will. Hurt people, hurt people. These people are hurting. I don't know what their particular hurt might be, but it's there somewhere. Hurt people need prayer. So we pray for those who would see us fail. Yup, as strange as that sounds, that is what we are called to do. We also need to understand that what they are doing is an emotional reaction to something. Emotional reactions and decisions are very rarely well thought out and rational. Trying to reason with a person who is in the midst of emotion is a fool's errand. This goes back to "Show Up and Shut Up". Just let them vent. Then pray. Then pray. Then pray some more. You may never see them heal. But in all of your own time in prayer, you will see yourself..

--Rise Up!!

===============================

"'You have heard that it was said, "Eye for eye, and tooth for tooth." But I tell you, do not resist an evil person. If anyone slaps you on the right cheek, turn to them the other cheek also. 40 And if anyone wants to sue you and take your shirt, hand over your coat as well.'"

-Matthew 5:38-40

Meditation thoughts:
　　Am I able to turn the other cheek?
　　What is my personal line for seeking '"justice"?
　　What foe do I need to pray for?

Prayer:
　　"Dear Jesus, people have attacked me. When I was attacked, it hurt me and I wanted justice.

Lord, you know my enemy. Please help me to find forgiveness for them. Put them in a positive light in my eyes. Show me their hurts so that I can pray for their healing. Please take away from me any desire for revenge. Bless my enemy beyond measure, Lord. I pray this in the powerful name of Jesus, Amen."

Day 36

Horse Latitudes (7.11.2016)

I'm not sure if you're familiar with the concept of the "horse latitudes". Back in the days of trans-Atlantic sailing they would hit areas called doldrums. These were found around the equator where the prevailing winds tend to go calm. No wind isn't necessarily a bad thing, unless you are counting on the winds to propel your vessel. Ships would lose their momentum and just begin to drift or just lay still - dead in the water - until the wind came again. With little to no propulsion the sailors would often jettison any extra weight that was being carried in order to get the boats going again. This often meant that non-critical supplies were tossed into the oceans. Sadly, the equine units aboard often fell into the "non-critical" classification and the horses would be sacrificed in order to save weight, hence the name "horse latitudes".

Sometimes in my recovery I can hit these areas where there seems to be a lack of wind in my sails. I feel like I am pushing through and making great strides toward my goals and then out of nowhere everything just stops moving and I come to a halt in the middle of the sea. It can be tough to get moving again.

I suppose the biggest danger is in assessing what is critical and non-critical at those times so that I can shed the proper ballast that impedes my progress. The temptation to just start grabbing things and tossing them over the rails can be strong. Water is extremely heavy by volume, but it is also a critical part of the voyage. From a recovery standpoint I might need to relinquish friends and relationships that drag me down. I might need to cut back on the amount of things I do at work. I may need to say "no" where I really want to say "yes" (ahhh, the joy of being co-dependent!).

Whatever it is, I know that when I hit these doldrums in life I need to make some changes. So here's to Spring Cleaning in July; here's to recovery; and here's to you as well!

--Rise Up!!

================================

"Create in me a pure heart, O God, and renew a steadfast spirit within me."

-Psalms 51:10

Meditation thoughts:

What ballast do I see in my life?
What has caused me to find the doldrums?
How will I gain momentum again?

Prayer:

"Dear Jesus, when my life, walk, and ministry come to a halt I need you to remind me of my purpose. Lord, I cannot see the things that drag me down on my own. Please reveal the dead weight in my life. Help me to remove myself from the people, places, and things that hold me back. I pray this in the powerful name of Jesus, Amen."

Day 37

Access Granted (8.8.2016)

This weekend I was able to participate in a kind of renewal for a dear friend. Like so many of us, he has been through some issues in the past. Since it is pretty much impossible to go through things in a vacuum, the people who have been around have either found out the facts, or more often than not, made up their own to fit what they think may be true. If this has never happened to you, you can probably quit reading now and move back over to Facebook! For the rest of us, read on...

Because of the amount of "new truth" that folks have so generously spread, my friend has found it difficult to have his ministry thrive in the way that it used to. Yes, it's not uncommon for people to hold our past (or perceived past) against us. This person is a gifted speaker who has had their voice quieted in the past few years. But this weekend was a triumph! During conversations that he had with his small group he mentioned that one of his dreams was to speak in the church where he was saved back in the 70's. After some inspired conversations with the right people, a date was set and he was invited to do just that. So Sunday a handful of us took a three and a half hour drive to go watch him preach. It was beautiful. "Amens" were said. People shouted "that's right!". We even heard a few people issue a familiar "Come ON!". Redemption. Restoration. Recovery.

This can be ours for the taking. We don't need to be repressed by our past, that's just following a lie from the enemy. Many times this lie is told loudest in the places where we live by people who think they know us. Listen folks, and hear this: I am not the things that I have done in the past; they do not define me even though people try to make it be that way. I am a grateful Christian believer. I am an heir to the kingdom. I am a Child of God! That's who and what I am. We might never soar in the places where we live (but I won't give up trying). But we will...

--Rise Up!!

=================================

"...when you heard about Christ and were taught in him in accordance with the truth that is in Jesus. You were taught, with regard to your former way of life, to put off your old self, which is being corrupted by its deceitful desires; to be made new in the attitude of your minds; and to put on the new self, created to be like God in true righteousness and holiness."

-Ephesians 4:21-24

Meditation thoughts:

What hurt have I allowed to hold me back?
What have I done to move beyond the things that hold me back?
How will people see me as I move in God's light?

Prayer:

"Dear Jesus, thank you for my new name. You see the good in me that the world chooses to deny. You see in me a person that I even overlook. I belong to you, and you alone. I am not the things that I have done, whether good or bad. I am your child. I pray this in the powerful name of Jesus, Amen."

Day 38

A Song of Ascents (1.6.2020)

Sometimes I wake up with a song or a thought in my head. Today, it's a thought that keeps rattling through my mind.

Let me step back for a moment. Starting at about 10 o'clock last night, I began having a spasm in my left ear drum. It was a maddening fluttering noise and feeling that wouldn't seem to stop, regardless of what I did. I changed positions as I sat on the couch watching TV. I went out to the garage and put finishing touches on the paint for some cabinets I am painting for a friend. I even did the unthinkable and went to bed! Nothing seemed to affect it. Finally I drifted off to sleep knowing that it would pass during the night and I would wake up a free man.

Nope

2 am...still going. 5 am...still going. 7 am...you guessed it, still there! And that's where my thought comes into the story. As I lay there wondering what I could do to remedy this situation I pondered the possibilities. The idea that seemed to gain favor with every passing minute of my torture was a meat

thermometer in the ear! But then I remembered *Psalms* 121:2-3 which goes like this:

"I lift my eyes to the hills -- where does my help come from? My help comes from the Lord, the Maker of heaven and earth."

Now one short prayer later and I'm able to put the thermometer back in the drawer. My ear is back to normal. All I needed to do was lean on God and...

--Rise Up!!

================================

"I lift my eyes to the hills -- where does my help come from? My help comes from the Lord, the Maker of heaven and earth."

-Psalms 121:2-3

Meditation thoughts:

What am I allowing to become a distraction in my life?
What have I done to change this distraction?
How can I put more trust in God?

Prayer:

"Dear Jesus, thank you for helping me to overcome all things. I know that you are my source of help, but I have turned to other places and things. Please forgive me. Help me in my unbelief. I know that when I trust in you, nothing is impossible. I pray this in the powerful name of Jesus, Amen."

Day 39

I Can't (6.22.2020)

How often have I said "I can't..."? Probably way more than even I think! This weekend we had a lot of time with "I can't" when we took our grandsons hiking in the Sierras.

Our oldest grandson is a kid with boundless energy. His younger brother is a bit more laid back. These character traits expressed themselves as soon as I called to invite them. One was all in, the other...not so much.

The morning of the hike was not too bad. We had a great car trip up to the mountains. We stopped at a store and got a bit of lunch to take on the hike. Smiles and laughter were plentiful. Then we headed up into the mountains and still, all was good with the world.

It wasn't until about one tenth of a mile into our hike that things turned sour for the younger guy. Yeah, one tenth of a mile into a four mile round trip. Oh boy, this was gonna be great!

As always, there were a lot of options on the table. I could let him quit and just sit in the car, but that was not really a good choice. Several hours alone in a parking lot in the mountains would be worse than the hike. He didn't know that, but we all did. Next option was to just push forward and let him catch up. Again, leaving a kid in the woods seems to be a bit of bad judgement. I decided to let Grammy and the oldest boy go on ahead while I stayed back with my daughter and him.

It was slow going. He absolutely did not think he could do it. Every 100 feet along the trail he was ready to quit. He tried reasoning with us that he would be fine all alone and we could get him on the way down. He tried pleading with us to just turn around and be done. He got mad and said mean things. He cried and looked for pity. Basically, it was like dealing with a person in recovery! Funny how that works, right?!?

So my daughter and I played the role of good sponsors and helped him see how he was going to make it. We set short term goals and met them. Then we started setting longer goals. We stopped and looked at how far we had come. And we didn't let him give in to the temptation to quit.

Eventually (3 hours later!) we made it to the lake where we were going to eat. He did it. He knew that he had done something difficult and that he had overcome his desire to quit. He was proud of it too.

Then, just like recovery, we had to keep stepping. The trip down was just as much "fun".

No one said it was going to be easy in this life. In fact, it's pretty common to hear the opposite. Just remember that you can do it, with the help of your people and God. Don't quit before you...

--Rise Up!!

================================

"You need to persevere so that when you have done the will of God, you will receive what he has promised."

-Hebrews 10:36

Meditation thoughts:
    What is the thing that makes you say "I can't"?
    What can you do to find victory?
    How will you celebrate your victory?

Prayer:

"Dear Jesus, I can't. I just don't know how I can. I feel helpless and alone. Jesus, you are my strength when I am weak, I know this. But I also need you to make me weak when I feel strong, because I need you to be the guide in my life; I am not as good as you. I am not as strong as you. I love you for your strength, please help me to accept becoming weak. I pray this in the powerful name of Jesus, Amen."

Day 40

Superb Owl (2.4.2019)

I heard last week that a lot of people got the wrong information when they did a web search for the Super Bowl. It seems that in the haste of flying thumbs and fingers the space got transposed so there were an inordinate number of searches for "Superb owl". It's a pretty understandable mistake and apparently it's an easy one to make as well.

How many times in life have I been led down the wrong path because I made a simple mistake? When I look for the wrong thing, most of the time I will probably find the wrong thing! That's why it is so important for me to maintain my walk with diligence. When I get lazy, it gets crazy. Hebrews 12:1 is a great reminder: "let us run with perseverance the race marked out for us,". Every day I need to keep looking forward, I need to focus on the important things, I need to work my steps. Then, and only then, am I able to...

--Rise Up!!

==================================

"Therefore, since we are surrounded by such a great cloud of witnesses, let us throw off everything that hinders and the sin that so easily entangles. And let us run with perseverance the race marked out for us, fixing our eyes on Jesus, the pioneer and perfecter of faith."

-Hebrews 12:1-2

Meditation thoughts:
What have I searched for in error?
How do I recognize my mistakes?
How can I stay more diligent?

Prayer:
"Dear Jesus, thank you for the mistakes in my life. Thank you for the ability to recognize these mistakes. I ask you to help me to learn from them and to use them as an avenue to becoming more like you. I pray this in the powerful name of Jesus, Amen."

Afterword

The Dishes

I love a good cup of coffee. There's just something therapeutic about it. The aroma, the taste, the feel of it. When everything is going crazy around me, that coffee helps to ground me and bring the world into focus.

Every event needs some preparation and also some clean up. For me, the art of coffee includes the theatre of brewing. I love the ritual of making a cup of Turkish coffee for friends. Heating of the water in the ibrik, grinding of the beans, adding spices…all of it culminating in the pour and that first sip. Ahhhh…

Then there's the dishes. I don't enjoy doing dishes. Some people do, and that's fine. It just isn't my thing. We've had our 40 cups and now we need to do some clean up.

When I started this blog in 2015 someone questioned whether or not I had the discipline needed in order to stay consistent with such an endeavor. So far, so good, but I haven't done it on my own. I have several people who have been with me on this journey from the start. There is a core group of readers who leave comments from time to time. I won't take the time and space to mention them by name, because at my age, I am certain to forget someone and I don't want to do that. You know who you are, and just know that you keep me going on the Monday mornings when I just don't feel like doing it one more time.

I hope that this 40 day journey has been helpful to you. I have enjoyed revisiting those old words from down the years. Sometimes I would smile as I read an old post. Sometimes my mind would jump to what I should have said next only to find out that that was exactly what I did say!

It brought back memories and it made me smile. A lot of times it made me think. I was proud of some of the things in there. Yet then again, some of them (those that didn't make the cut) made me cringe. I never thought I'd get through all of this but here we are. Yes, this is the end of another book, so I suppose the only thing left to do is…

–Rise Up!!

About the Author

Paul Pippen was released from incarceration in 2002. He began working on his own recovery in 2003. He has been active as a missionary to prisons for Celebrate Recovery, Prison Fellowship, and Messed Up Ministries since 2018. You can read his weekly blog at MinisterOfMocha.com. He also hosts the Mess it Up podcast. The loves of his life are his wife, Bev, their four children and numerous grandchildren. Paul is an avid fan of the LA Kings and the Arsenal.

More from Paul Pippen

Paul's books can be found on Apple Books, Kindle, and in paperback.

Still in Beta
https://www.amazon.com/dp/B086VSPW83
http://books.apple.com/us/book/id1508817971

Peace by Piece
https://www.amazon.com/dp/B09RT4FWPN
http://books.apple.com/us/book/id1608524016

Finding Your "ing"
https://a.co/d/hmuFTIL
https://books.apple.com/us/book/finding-your-ing/id6447341232

Hookers in Heaven
https://a.co/d/57lk3Ms

Made in the USA
Monee, IL
15 February 2025